AF430836

Letters from Luis

The First Four Exhibits:
Trompe l'Oeil
Qin Shi
The Promise of al Toman
Games

Written by Tim Pingelton, PhD
Illustrations by Sophie Pingelton

Table of Contents

Hola! My name is Luis, and I live in an art museum in a town called Tarapoto, Peru with my mother and sister, María. The museum is on the bottom floor, and we live above it on the second floor. The museum is called Museo Cautivador, which means "captivating museum" in English. My mom, who I call Mami, knows a lot about art, and people all over the world know her. She runs the museum; this job is called a curator, and it means that she also picks out the art to show. There isn't much permanent art in the museum, but Mami's friends like to bring art from their museums and show it for a while at Museo Cautivador.

The art is not just painting but also sculpture, textiles, or even architecture. And sometimes we show one kind of art or one style but have examples from all over the world.

I wrote these letters to share exciting and mysterious stories of the visiting exhibitions we have at the museum. You might even learn something, like I did.

Trompe l'Oeil

"Madagascan Day Gecko" by Bernard Spragg

Tarapoto, Peru

Hola Amigo,

Believe it or not, living with Mami and my little sister María in our apartment above this cool museum gets a little boring at times. To entertain myself, I've been telling Maria that the geckos (which are little green lizards) that sometimes climb up the walls of our rooms at night are poisonous. Really, they are totally harmless and pretty funny, but Maria got scared. She couldn't sleep that night and told Mami what I was telling her. Mami got mad and made me go outside and kick the soccer ball against the back wall of the museum. She's the coach of my soccer team, and I'm not that great. I still can't get the ball to

go where I want it to go all the time.

It was really boring, kicking against that boring wall. Then Mami came out and told me she had a surprise for me. It wasn't much of a surprise, though, because the surprise was that her old friend Frederick van der Horst was coming to stay for a week. Professor van der Horst visits every year, and every time he brings some crazy stuffed birds or dusty old letters or something. He is a short, chubby guy, but he always smiles and listens to what I say. He has an art museum in the Netherlands, which is a country over by Germany and Belgium. Usually, Mami and Professor van der Horst sit around drinking tea and talking about art and their adventures around the world.

Professor van der Horst usually stays in my room, and I have to sleep down on the first floor, where the museum is. This time, though, Mami said the professor would stay in "the back room." This room is always totally empty except for a few cardboard boxes.

Well, when I came back from school last Tuesday, Professor van der Horst was sipping tea on the back porch with Mami. Maria was sipping apple juice from a tippy cup. The first

6

thing the professor asked me was if I have been nice to Maria. I looked at Maria, and she smiled.

"It's not nice to scare people, Luis," he said, "because sometimes you end up the one being scared." He always talks mysteriously like that.

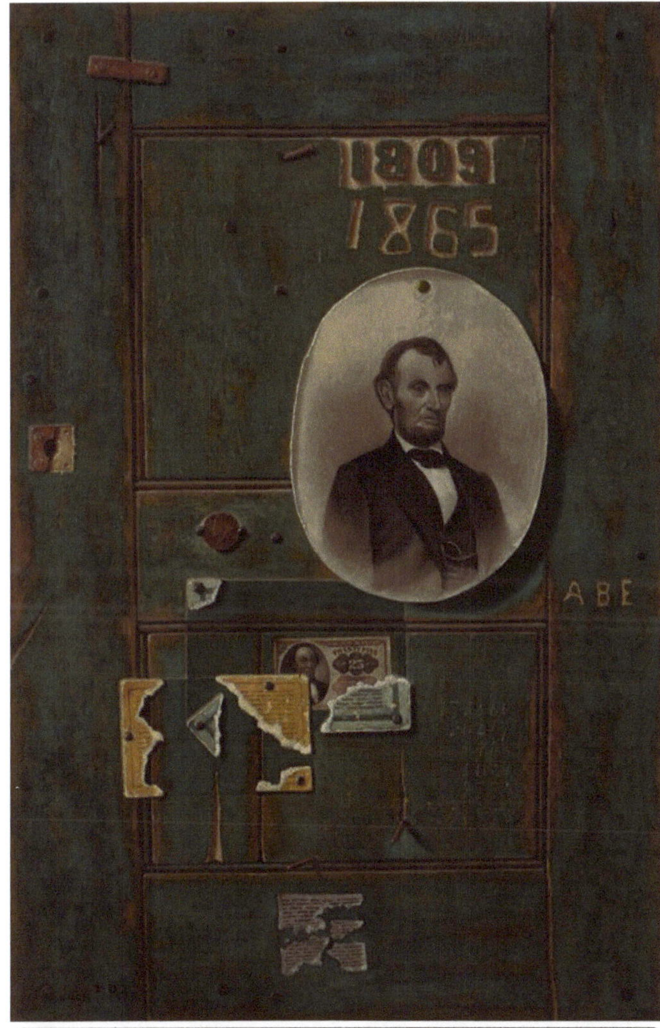

Remimiscences of 1865, 1904 · John Frederick Peto · Minneapolis Institute of Art (The Julia B. Bigelow Fund by John Bigelow)

I went up to the fourth floor, where we live, and I noticed the door to "the back room" was a little open. I walked down the hall and peeked in. That room that is usually empty had tons of crazy things in it. It

was a little dark in the room, but, as I stepped inside, I noticed a painting of a serious guy with a beard, and there were flies everywhere. It was gross. I saw another painting of a serious guy with a bigger beard. There was also a painting with words in a foreign language, and, of course, there were bugs sitting on it. The professor's room was a complete mess. He also carved into the closet door and stuck up a picture of Abraham Lincoln. Mami was not going to be happy about that.

The guy also stuck papers in a rack on the wall or even stuck them to the wall itself! Most incredible of all were the violins hanging all over the place. Even in the bathroom!

Portrait of a Carthusian, 1446 · Petrus Christus · Metropolital Museum of Art, New York (The Jules Bache Collection, 1949)

Portrait of a Carthusian (detail), 1446 · Petrus Christus · Metropolital Museum of Art, New York (The Jules Bache Collection, 1949)

St. Jerome (detail), c. 1470 · Francesco Benaglio · The National Gallery of Art, New York (Samuel H. Kress Collection)

And in the little shelf on each wall, he put big bunches of flowers. One of the bunches attracted more bugs and even a couple of geckos. Professor van der Horst brought a bunch of stuff and hung it up on the walls! One painting was even hanging backwards! I slowly walked around the room, gazing at these fantastic old things.

Then I heard a sharp hiss … My spine tingled and I froze.

St. Jerome, c. 1470 · Francesco Benaglio · The National Gallery of Art, New York (Samuel H. Kress Collection)

Letter Board, 1666-1668 · Samuel Dirksz van Hoogstraten ·
Staatliche Kunsthalle, Karlsruhe, Germany

Trompe l'Oeil, 19th C. · Carl Dietrich · Minneapolis Institute of
Art (Bequest of Professor Alfred Moir)

The Reverse of a Framed Painting, after 1675 · Cornelius Norbertus Gijsbrechts · Statens Museum for Kunst, Copenhagen, Denmark

I slowly turned and saw an antique gold cup sitting on a little shelf in the wall. I didn't remember that shelf. What really startled me, though, was the evil red-eyed snake in the cup! The snake froze, too, probably wondering where it should bite me. I took one slow step backward toward the door, and then I took another step.

I got out of that room, tripped over that crazy lion statue in the hallway, and stumbled down to the porch. Mami was just sitting down when I got there. Mami, Maria, and Professor van

Chalice of St. John, 1480 · Hans Memling · Statens National Gallery of Art, Washington, DC

der Horst all looked so calm sitting there when there was a vicious snake in "the back room."

I couldn't talk at first, and Mr. van der Horst pulled back a chair for me to sit in. I finally told them what I saw, but Mami seemed totally calm.

"What were you doing in our guest's room, Luis?" she asked.

"I don't know. I was just going to my room," I said. "But what are you going to do about the snake? It could be anywhere by now!"

Maria laughed. Mami said, "Luis, that snake hasn't moved in over 500 years. Come with me."

Then we all went back up to "the back room." Mami carried Maria. I told her to watch out, but she walked right in the room and opened the drapes. All that crazy stuff was still all over the place. I reached over to flick the fly that was on the frame of one of those bearded guys, and I realized why Mami and Mr. van der Horst were laughing. I looked close and realized the fly was actually painted on the frame. In fact, the frame was not a real frame but just part of the painting. All the flies around the room were painted on the paintings. The flies were painted to look like they were real flies sitting on the paintings. It was totally cool.

Even the violins were just really good paintings. And the letters and all that other stuff. Then I looked over at that snake, still ready to strike from its golden cup. Mami laughed.

"It's OK, Luis. The snake is painted. Look closely, even the little shelf it's on is painted. And the shadows. The canvas of the painting is totally flat. It's called trompe l'oeil." [Pronounced "tromp loy]

Large Flower Piece with Imperial Crown, 1624 · Roelant Savery · Central Museum, Utrecht, Germany

Two Laughing Girls, 1880 · Pere Borrell del Caso · Bank of Spain Headquarters, Madrid, Spain

"Yes," said Professor van der Horst, chuckling, "trompe l'oeil is French for 'fool the eye.' Painting like that takes a lot of skill. The artists work to create the optical illusion of three dimensions in their paintings. You, my dear boy, were fooled by these old painters just like you fooled little María into thinking those harmless geckos are poisonous." María smiled.

He pulled another print from his briefcase. "Here is another one by the same painter. Look at how the girl's elbow appears to stick outside of the frame, as if there really were two girls in the frame and they could come out into where you are like that guy in the last painting. Pretty incredible, huh? It fooled your eyes, yes?"

Escaping Criticism, 1874 · Pere Borrell del Caso · Bank of Spain Headquarters, Madrid, Spain

Chalice of St. John (detail), 1480 · Hans Memling · Statens National Gallery of Art, Washington, DC

He pulled a print from his briefcase. "Here is a print of a famous work of trompe l'oeil. On the wall, it looks like that guy is coming out of the frame into the room you are in. The artist created this effect by using shadow and perspective masterfully. And doesn't it look like you could touch that other girl's fingertip? It is hard to look at this artwork and believe that it is painted on a flat surface."

"Yeah, but what about the hiss? I heard that snake hiss." I said.

Mami said, "Well, my son, when I saw you enter our friend's room, I could not resist the temptation to give you a little scare. I hissed and then ran back down here and told everyone what I did."

Everyone laughed, and I felt like a fool. I went outside and kicked the soccer ball against the wall some more. Then I got a great idea. I got some chalk and drew a few things on the wall, so it looked like a World Cup goalie was guarding the goal. I drew in a big crowd in the background and a scoreboard showing a 2 to 2 tie with 1 second left in the game. I kicked all afternoon, and now I'm pretty good. The ball goes where I want it to now. At least most of the time.

I also told Maria the truth about those harmless geckos. And I told her I was sorry.

Never a moment's peace here at Museo Cautivador. Well, I'll write again soon.

Your Amigo,

Luis

Qin Shi

Terrocotta Officer, c. 210 BCE
· Unknown Crafters · Qin Shi
Huangdi Museum, Shaanxi,
China

Tarapoto, Peru

Hola Amigo,

How are you doing? I had to go to the hospital a week ago.

Actually, I had to go twice. You remember how extra safe my mom is? Well, I left our apartment (on the top floor of the Museo Cautivador) and started walking down the staircase to where the exhibits are. I was eating a bagel as I was walking, and I tripped over my feet and rolled down a whole flight of stairs. I felt OK, but Mami saw me fall, and she screamed like a fire alarm.

As you know, she is the director (or "curator") of the museum, so she felt like she had to be in charge. She told me not to move a muscle, and I stopped reaching out for the bagel that was inches away from my fingertips. Then she wrapped my whole upper body in towels (like the mummy of Queen Al-Tomar) and took me to the hospital. The doctors checked me out and said I was OK, but Mami made them X-ray my head.

The nurse said they X-ray all kinds of things...even animals and art objects. It took forever, and, of course, the X-ray showed that my head was not broken.

Anyway, I have got a story to tell you—a Chinese army invaded our little museum in the foothills of the Andes Mountains here in Peru. And the soldiers are more than 2200 years old! My mom won the battle, and you will find out how she did it.

The First X-Ray—Mrs. Rontgen's Hand, 1895 · X-Ray Radiograph by William Rontgen · U.S. National Library of Medicine, Bethesda, Maryland

Terracotta Soldiers, c. 210 BCE · Unknown Crafters · Qin Shi Huangdi Museum, Shaanxi, China (Photo by Immanuel Giel)

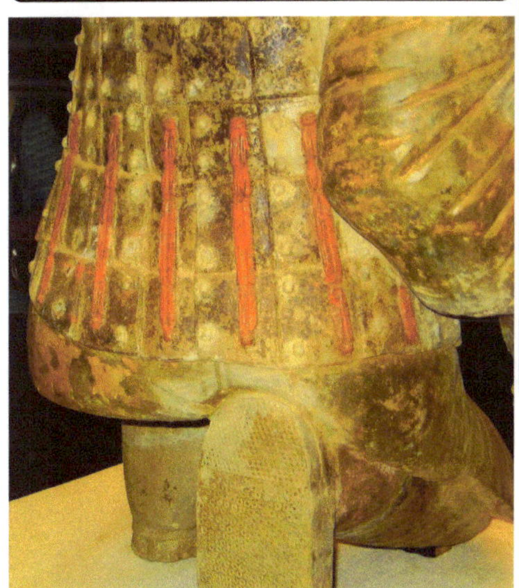

Terracotta Archer, c. 210 BCE · Unknown Crafters · Qin Shi Huangdi Museum, Shaanxi, China (Photo by Tomasz Sienicki, Commons. Wikimedia.org) Above and left.

First of all, the soldiers are part of an exhibit on loan to the museum from China. About 30 years ago, some farmers were digging a well in eastern China, and they hit pottery in the shape of a head. They dug down some more and found the rest of the body. Then they dug some more and found another pottery statue. The statues were both wearing ancient Chinese battle gear and held real weapons. The farmers called some friends over, and they dug a lot more.

Portrait of Qin Shi Huangdi, 18th C. · Anonymous artist · British Library, London

Terracotta Soldiers, c. 210 BCE (Coloring recreated) · Unknown Crafters · Qin Shi Huangdi Museum, Shaanxi, China

Terracotta Charioteer and Horses, c. 210 BCE · Unknown Crafters · Qin Shi Huangdi Museum, Shaanxi, China

They eventually found 8000 statues— soldiers, horses, chariots—made to guard the burial place of Qin Shi Huang ["chin sure hwong"], who died in 206 B.C.E. and who was the first emperor of China. Qin Shi is famous for starting the building of the Great Wall of China.

A few weeks ago, my mom talked to the curator of the museum that was built over the spot where those farmers originally dug for a well, and she eventually convinced the curator to send two pottery warriors, four pottery horses, and some small items from the excavation to our museum.

Mami was really excited about this because these ancient soldiers rarely leave China. Each one is a little different—can you imagine how long it must have taken to create all those different life-size statues?!

Each soldier has a different facial expression and hair styling! Mami was interested in this because she liked the way they combined art, history, and the art-making process. The guy from China was also bringing about 100 pottery soldiers that were made in a factory so he could sell them at our museum. The new pottery soldiers are the exact same size as the real ancient soldiers.

Terracotta Soldiers, c. 210 BCE · Unknown Crafters · Qin Shi Huangdi Museum, Shaanxi, China (Photo by Tomasz Sienicki, Commons.Wikimedia.org)

As I said before, my mom likes to be in charge of things, but, well, sometimes she gets a little confused. The fake pottery army came first (the pottery is really called terracotta, which is Latin for "cooked earth"—both the ancient and new soldiers were made from clay and sand that was shaped and then baked). A typical reddish flowerpot is made of terracotta.

Mami picked up the Chinese curator at the airport. When they got back, I told the Chinese curator the fake terracotta soldiers looked ancient, but he laughed at me. "Do not be silly, little boy," he said. "Emperor Qin made sure his real soldiers were made better than that." I didn't like being called "little boy," but maybe that's what older people call kids in China.

When the real soldiers came the next day, I still couldn't tell the difference, but the curator from the Qin Terra Cotta Army Museum treated the real soldiers like they were gold. Speaking of gold—there was hardly any. That's a big mystery about the terracotta army.

Emperor Qin had two bronze chariots made, but no gold was found. Sure, the terra cotta soldiers are priceless, but a little gold would be nice, too.

Originally, the soldiers were also painted, but after being buried in the ground for 2000 years, the paint is almost all gone. One of the soldiers here at the museum still has purple paint on it. The curator from China told me that the purple paint was super difficult to make because it required certain rocks to be ground into a fine powder, mixed a certain way, and heated super hot. Scientists today are not sure how people back then got the mixture that hot (1000°C, 1900°F!). It's a mystery. Also, when the soldiers were dug out of the ground, the air caused the purple to disappear most of the time, so archaeologists left more statues in the ground. Scientists know they were once painted purple by using special lighting.

The curator had to fly to Brazil later that day, and my mom promised him the soldiers would be fine and the exhibit would open to the public in three days, when the Chinese curator was supposed to return. I rode along when Mami took the Chinese curator to the airport.

In the car coming back from the airport, Mami asked me, "Luis, where did that curator put the fake terracotta soldiers?"

"He put them in the Restoration Vault. Why?"

"Um, because that's where I put the REAL soldiers, too," she said. She sped the car up and said, "So it seems the new cheap fake ones are mixed up with the real priceless ones!"

The restoration vault is a special room where works of art are repaired—the room is like a big bank vault. It took Mami four tries to open the combination locks, and she threw open the vault door.

There were about 100 soldiers staring at us—all of them seemed completely identical!

Gold Clothing Ornaments, c. 210 BCE · Unknown Crafters · Qin Shi Huangdi Exhibition in Thailand, 2019 (Photo by Trisorn Triboon)

My mom carefully stepped around the soldiers, trying to find the real, priceless two. It was no use.

The phone rang, and I went to get it. It was the curator from China. He wanted to know how the real soldiers were doing. I told him everything was fine, and I asked him what the difference between the real ones and the fake ones was. "Well, little boy," he said. "The real ones are made out of 2200-year-old terra cotta, and the fakes are made of new plaster made to look like ancient terra cotta." I asked him more about the difference, but all he said was that new plaster weighs a lot more than the old terra cotta. Then I had a brilliant idea of how we could tell the real ones from the fakes. Do you know what it was?

Well, I went back to my mom and told her what the Chinese curator told me. Then I told her we could tell the real ones from the fakes by weighing them all. The fakes would be a lot heavier. Mami immediately scooted over a big scale, and I helped her carefully set one after another soldier on the scale to weigh them all. We wore white gloves to protect the priceless statues. It took all night. I wrote down the weights. Maria ended up falling asleep on a pile of packing blankets from the moving truck that brought the soldiers.

Guess what—every soldier weighed the same. Why did they all weigh the same? Shouldn't the real soldiers weigh less?

We were supposed to pick up the Chinese curator at noon the next day, and it was almost midnight. Mami brought down some cookies and milk. I told her I was going up to bed, and I grabbed a cookie on my way out of the restoration vault.

I looked back at the vault, and Mami was staring at me with a sad look on her face. Then I tripped on the bottom stair and bit my tongue. Mami ran over to me with a wild look in her eye.

"Luis, you are a clumsy little genius!" she shouted. She ran past me up the stairs. I yelled, "Mami, where are you going?"

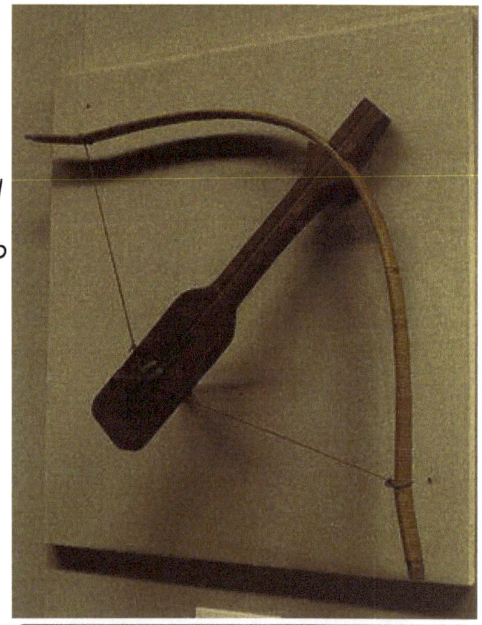

Qin-Era Crossbow, c. 210 BCE · Unknown Crafter · Shaanxi History Museum

"I'm getting my shoes. We have to go to the hospital for X-rays," she yelled back.

"But mom, I barely tripped. I'm fine," I said to her as she came back downstairs while pulling on her shoes.

"That's good, son," she said.

"Then why are you taking me to get another X-ray?"

She laughed. Then she said, "You're not getting the X-ray—they are." She pointed to the 102 soldiers looking out from the restoration vault.

To make a long story short, after the 34th X-ray, we found out why the real statues weighed more than they should have. The 34th soldier was filled with jewels and gold foil! It was one of the two real soldiers. We found the other one on the 39th x-ray. Ancient Chinese emperors usually had gold foil covering their burial furniture, but I guess Emperor Qin wanted gold inside the soldiers, for whatever reason.

Maria and I were sound asleep when we reached the airport to pick up the Chinese curator, but Mami was wide awake. She skipped out of the car, bursting to tell the Chinese curator about this momentous discovery.

The curator was indeed amazed, and he told us more about Qin Shi's burial place.

Someone at that time (again, way over 2000 years ago) wrote that, buried deep in the ground, Qin Shi is actually buried with all kinds of jewels and gold. A river of mercury was dug around the tomb because Qin Shi thought mercury could help keep his spirit alive. It is a poisonous liquid, and that is part of the reason his tomb has not been dug out yet.

Also, lots of cross-bows were loaded and set up as traps for anyone who enters the lower burial chamber. So there's that.

Well, that's the story from your friend in Peru. I'll try not to fall down stairs any time soon.

Your Amigo,

Luis

The Promise of al Toman

Terrocotta Officer, c. 210 BCE
· Unknown Crafters · Qin Shi
Huangdi Museum, Shaanxi,
China

Tarapoto, Peru

Hola Amigo,

Well, my friend, it's been another interesting month at the museum.

Sometimes even boring times can be good if you think about it--even waiting at a restaurant while my mom and sister finish eating or standing around at the museum can be interesting if I play a game my father taught me. I always ask myself "why."

For example, there is a display of smashed up TVs mixed up with hundreds of wires in the museum. Why? Because someone thinks it's art. Why? Because it makes them think of something. Why? Because they've never seen TVs like that before. Why? Because the TV is usually something that we take care not to smash up. Why? Because a lot of people think television is precious, more precious than music or kickball. Now that's interesting.

Egyptian Court, photo c. 1859 CE · Photo by Phillip Henry Delamotte · Metropolitan Museum of Art, New York (Gilman Collection Museum Purchase, 2005)

Egyptian Court, photo c. 1859 CE · Photo by Phillip Henry Delamotte · Metropolitan Museum of Art, New York (Gilman Collection Museum Purchase, 2005)

Anyway, we had a mummy's curse come true here at the museum— kind of. Let me explain

My mom (I call her Mami, and she's the curator, or director, of Museo Cautivador) managed to get a museum in Egypt to loan her a mummy, statues, some gold necklaces and other things from a tomb in Egypt. This tomb was discovered by Ground Penetrating Radar—that's radar on planes flying high

•Mummy Mask, c. 1353 BCE · Unknown Crafters · Metropolitan Museum of Art, New York (Rogers Fund, 1918) [Above]
•Linen Wrapping from the Mummy of Amenhotep III, c. 1353 BCE · Unknown Crafters · The Egyptian Museum of Art, Cairo (Photo in Catalogue Général des Antiquités égyptiennes, 1908) [Left]

overhead that can actually see about 12 feet into the ground. Isn't that cool?!

The museum was all set up so it looked like a pharaoh's tomb in Egypt. A pharaoh was a ruler in Egypt a couple thousand years ago. Mami also adjusted the lighting to make the museum look kind of mysterious. It was pretty cool.

The mummy's coffin (called the sarcophagus) has been in a museum in England for about a hundred years, and the mummy and the sarcophagus have not been together in 150 years. A curator from The British Museum is bringing the sarcophagus to our museum. It is supposed to weigh about ten tons, but the mummy weighs only as much as you or me. The mummy had not ever left Egypt. The mummy came in the back of a big rental truck from Lima. She (it's a girl mummy) was wrapped in all kinds of protective packaging and stuff. I didn't see the mummy wrappings until the mummy mask and all the packing stuff was removed. She's never been unwrapped, which is a big deal

Necklace with the Head of Egyptian God Bes, c. 6-4th C BCE · Unknown Goldsmith · Metropolitan Museum of Art, New York (Dodge Fund, 1965)

because she died about 5000 years ago. The curator from the Cairo Museum in Egypt came along with her. He wasn't a mummy (ha ha).

Sarcophagus of Hathor Priestess Henhenet, c. 2051-2030 BCE · Unknown Crafters · Metropolitan Museum of Art, New York (Gift of Egypt Exploration Fund, 1907)

Unexplored Entrance to a Royal Tomb, photo c. 1860 bu Zangaki · Unknown Crafters · Thebes, Greece (Photo New York Public Library (The Miriam and Ira Wallach Division))

Stela of the Son of Amenhotep III, 1353 BCE · Unknown Crafters · Egyptian Museum, Munich, Germany

The sarcophagus from England came later that day in another rental truck. There were real hieroglyphics all over her sarcophagus. A curator showed me a picture of what the mummy's tomb looked like when it was first discovered. While the curators from England and Egypt were shaking hands and inspecting the things, I asked Mami what the hieroglyphics on the sarcophagus said. She told me they said, "Queen Al-Toman is buried within." The curators stopped talking and looked at Mami.

I had a feeling that meant something important, but I didn't want to ask about it in front of Mami—she'd tell me to go back to our apartment on the top floor of the museum to do my homework. But I talked with the curators later when they took a coffee break—when Mami was checking on something else.

Statue of Queen/Pharaoh Cleopatra III, Prob. c.130 BCE · Unknown Crafters · The Walters Museum, Baltimore (Acquired by Henry Walters, 1928)

"So what does the sarcophagus really say," I asked the English curator.

"Your mother is right, it says…" he started to say. But I cut him off. "What else does it say?" I asked.

The Egyptian curator's hand shook, and he dropped his coffee cup.

It broke on the floor. He said, "It is bad. Very bad."

Neither of them would say more until I told the man from Egypt that he just broke a priceless Charles the First tea-cup (I guess he doesn't know his china dishware because I totally made up that Charles the First stuff). I said Mami would be furious at him but that I would take the blame for it if he would tell me what it really says.

Statuette of Lady Djehutynakht, 2010-1961 BCE · Unknown Crafter · The Harvard University, Boston (Museum of Fine Arts Expedition)

He said, "I will tell you what the sarcophagus says, but do not let it upset you. After all, in nearly 4000 years, the warning has not come to be."

"So what does it say?" I asked again. The Egyptian looked over at a big statue of Queen Al-Toman, but he would not speak. She looked nice to me, but the curator's face looked worried. The curator from the British Museum spoke up.

"It says, 'Disturb me from my sleep, ye people, and I will bury myself again.' It says that over and over, all over the sarcophagus. This frightens many people because there is always great mystery around mummies and ancient Egyptian burial practices."

Then we heard a deep rumbling sound that shook our clothes. I could tell the curators thought it was Queen Al-Toman, but I laughed because I knew it was the big tractor again, working in the side yard. Museo Cautivador got money to build a big new section so we can get even more traveling exhibits. The tractor driver was yelling "¿Donde?" to Mami to find out where to put his big load of soil. She couldn't hear over the loud tractor, so she just pointed to the old part of the museum that was opened.

They had to tear down a wall to connect up the new part they are building, and we are getting a new air conditioner unit while the wall is open. We have to get a really huge air conditioner because it is really humid here in this valley in the Andes Mountains, and the artwork rots and breaks if it gets too damp.

Bastet Statuette, c. 644-30 BCE · Unknown Crafter · Metropolitan Museum of Art, New York (Rogers Fund, 1958)

Stela of the Master Craftsman, Scribe, and Sculptor Irtysen, c. 2000 BCE · Carving by Irtysen · Louvre Museum, Paris

The new air conditioner will cool the museum and keep it drier than our air conditioner now. The one now is really big, but it doesn't dry the air as good as a new one will. The construction workers have been piling up dirt near the open wall, by the old air conditioner, because there's no other place to put the dirt.

Anyway, it took two days to move the mummy and her sarcophagus into the "Traveling Exhibits" space in the museum. They also brought in a ton of gold jewelry and other stuff that was buried with Queen Al-Toman. Every night, two guards stood at the open wall to make sure no one stole anything. No one stole anything those two nights, but we almost lost the whole museum a few nights later. But let me back up.

Again.

The day before Mami opened the exhibit to the public, she worked extra hard making sure everything was all right. She asked some guys to build a temporary wall so she wouldn't have to worry about guarding that area during the exhibit (they couldn't move out the dirt in time, so they left it in a pile outside). And I helped make sure the descriptions matched the piece of jewelry or whatever it described. Mami helped Hilda and Isabel polish the floors and set the lighting so everything would be perfect.

All these statues found in tombs made the museum seem creepier than usual, and I knew a lot of people would come. I also think the ancient Egyptian way of using hieroglyphic writing is cool, although I really don't know what it all says. The information card next to this gravestone-looking slab said it was a stela ["steela"], which is a carved stone used to show important news. This one says that the carver who made it is one of the best artists in the area and that he has secrets about how to mix chemicals that no one else knows. Which is cool.

It was supposed to be another hot day in

42

Tarapoto, Peru when the public would be admitted to the Queen Al-Toman exhibit. I followed my mom around the museum the night before the people from all over the world would come to see the mummy of Queen Al-Toman and her sarcophagus together for the first time in 150 years. After all, the queen spent about 3000 years in that coffin.

My mom checked everything. Twice. I was getting really tired, but she wanted me to follow her and check to see that everything was perfect. If the people liked the exhibit, maybe the museum would get more money to finish off the construction project and to get more art pieces. She readjusted the lighting,

The Bishop Museum at Night, 2017 · Photo by Tim Pingelton · Honolulu, Hawaii

repolished doorknobs, and rechecked that our old air conditioner was set just right to keep all the people cool.

She set it extra cool because there would be so many people that their bodies would heat the place up.

I shot out of bed the next morning because I heard Mami scream. I started running downstairs to the "Traveling Exhibits" rooms on the first floor, but I stopped at the top of the stairway. Everything — the polished floor, the display tables, Queen Al-Toman and her sarcophagus— everything was covered with dirt!

"She's burying herself again," I said to myself. It was true—the sarcophagus was totally covered in dirt, and she was taking the rest of the museum with her! Some people waiting to see the exhibit got in and stared at the incredible sight. Then the curator from Egypt broke through the crowd and stood in amazement.

"The curse of Al-Toman is coming true," he muttered. Someone gasped.

Mami was closest to the covered-up sarcophagus. She was standing in dirt up to her ankles, looking around her with a worried look. Everyone was silent, watching my mom, since she is the curator of Museo Cautivador.

"Señora Abrazo," the Egyptian curator said. "I must leave...we should all leave before Al-Toman buries us with her."

At that moment, a cool breeze drifted through the museum and more dirt showered down on us and everything. Some people screamed. Most people started heading for the exit. I felt scared, but I felt sad, too because I know how much time and effort my mom put into this exhibit. I dropped my head and frowned. Then I looked at my mom, and SHE WAS SMILING.

Then she started laughing. She laughed louder and louder.

Everyone stopped and looked at her.

"What is it, mate?" the curator from the British Museum asked.

My mom stopped herself from laughing, and she said in a serious voice, "I can stop the curse of Al-Toman!" People gasped. It was totally silent— except for the soft sound of dirt falling like snow.

Mami walked through the dirt over to a wall where some
of Al- Toman's jewelry was displayed. She reached toward a
statue of a mean-

looking hawk. But she reached past the jewelry display
case and leaned to the wall. She reached to the air conditioner
thermostat and turned the air conditioner off.

The dirt shower ended instantly.

"You see," Mami said with a laugh in her voice, "dirt is piled
up next to our air conditioner. When I set the air conditioner
on extra-cool last night, the blower sucked up the dirt and blew
it out through these vents." She pointed to the many air vents
around the museum.

People breathed a sigh of relief and cheered my mom. She
said to everyone, "Now if you all would please go to our terraza
with a splendid view of the Andes Mountains, we will serve café
and juice while I sweep up this dirt. The display will be clean
enough to view in about one hour. Perhaps the curators from
the Cairo Museum and the British Museum would share some
fascinating stories of mummies and Egyptian royalty?"

The British curator said "Sure," and the Egyptian curator,
finally breaking into a relaxed smile, said, "shall we start with
the Old Kingdom—perhaps the Third Dynasty?" The people
cheered again, and Mami and I got busy serving drinks and
cookies. Even little Maria helped by passing out napkins. Mom

got busy with the vacuum cleaner. The little layer of dirt on the sarcophagus and wraps of Al-Toman gave the exhibit a special, ancient feel, and, a couple of hours later, everyone left thinking Museo Cautivador is a very special place.

What is art? Well, I don't really know for sure. But I do know that I like those old Egyptian statues made out of wood or limestone. I also like Dutch paintings, comic strips, and drawings of birds. I'm not sure about those smashed TVs, but some people like them.

I have to study for a math test tomorrow, so I better start on that.

I'll write soon—there will probably be another mystery at the Museo Cautivador.

Su Amigo (Your Friend),

Luis

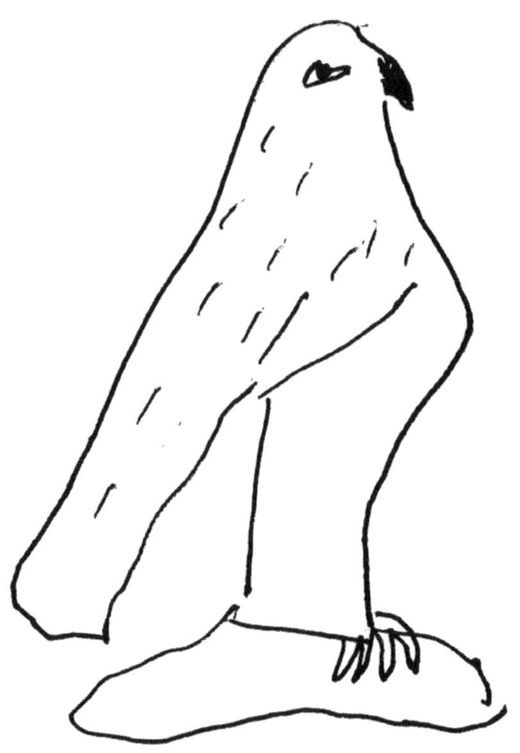

Knave of Horns, from The Cloisters Playing Cards, c. 1475 CE · Unknown Crafter · Metropolitan Museum of Art, New York (The Cloisters Collection, 1983)

Tarapoto, Peru

Hola Amigo,

I don't know about you, but sometimes in the summer I actually wish it was the school year instead of summer break. At least at school I can see my friends more, and there are a lot of things to do. I admit there are interesting things here, living in this museum in the foothills of the Andes Mountains in Peru, where my mother is the curator (she runs the museum). We always have visiting exhibits which are crazy in their own ways, but right now we are in between exhibits (the Qin Shi exhibit just got shipped back to Shannxi, China). Even after exploring around the area and riding my bike all over the place, I got so bored I have actually been playing games with my little sister Maria.

Lemme start with the exhibition that Mami is setting up now. It's mainly paintings from the National Gallery of Art in Washington, D.C. Mami knows the curator there, and every year some of their paintings and things come all the way here from D.C. for a few weeks. The exhibits are always cool, but still, this summer break seems to last FOREVER.

Anyway, the trucks came, and Mami and a bunch of people were unloading the paintings. Since Mami said that Maria and I were supposed to play outside (I think we were driving her crazy as she was trying to make sure none of the art pieces were damaged), my sister and I went out and made a new game. We called it Poke and Run, and the rules were that we were supposed to poke Mami and then run before she realized who poked her. We both had to do it at the same time; that was one of the rules. It worked for a while because she was focusing on unwrapping paintings and filling out paperwork, but she caught on to us pretty soon and got angry. She even ended up standing on a chair so that she could look over

the bushes around the museum and point to the field she wanted Maria to go to with our dog Pedro. She told me I had to first roll up the garden hose into a neat coil.

Later, Mami told Maria get the leash and bring in Pedro, and she talked to me.

She said, "Son, your sister is a little girl who is learning how people are supposed to act. I know that, living here in a pretty small town in Peru, you don't have a lot of friends. Especially during this summer break when you don't see your friends as much. Still, Maria looks up to you. It is part of your responsibility to help me raise her to be responsible and nice, as you are. I am always proud to introduce you to visiting museum directors and other important people. Please help me while we get this new exhibit set up. I'm really busy right now, but maybe later we can do something fun. Maybe go to Moyobamba and see that movie you were talking about. Let's go in—there are a few things I want to show you."

We went inside, and Mami took off er work gloves and dragged me in front of a painting that was just brought in. "Here's something that will keep you out of trouble for a little while," Mami said, "Sit down in front of this painting and imagine what is going on. Try to make a story about what is happening in the painting, and then come and tell me what you came up with. You can tell me in a little while." I sat and looked at the painting for a while, and soon Maria came with Pedro, and they joined me.

A Scene on the Ice, c. 1625 CE · Hendrick Avercamp · National Gallery of Art, Washington, D.C. (Alisa Mellon Bruce Fund)

It was an old-looking painting with a bunch of people walking on a frozen pond. And there was a windmill in the background. María started saying goofy stuff like "A circus came to this town in the winter—because the people are wearing those crazy clothes—and this is after the circus is over and the performers are going to the town to watch the people in the town like the town people watched them earlier." Crazy, right?

I told her "No, silly. That's the kind of clothes people wore then. This is probably somewhere in Europe, and they're just doing what people did then." But then I noticed two people in the painting carrying what looked a lot like a golf club. But he was walking or skating on ice. And there was a dog trying to run on the ice, which must have been kinda funny to see.

The movers put down another painting they just unwrapped near where we were, and it looked like another ice skating scene. It had a really fancy frame. I scooted over to that painting, and, although I could tell she was angry that I shot down her circus idea, Maria scooted over, too. So did Pedro.

This painting was a little different, but still old timey.

A Scene on the Ice (detail), c. 1625 CE · Hendrick Avercamp · National Gallery of Art, Washington, D.C. (Alisa Mellon Bruce Fund)

What was interesting, though, was that there were more guys holding what looked like golf clubs. Or maybe hockey sticks, but not quite. One guy was about to fall down, and he was probably going to bring his girlfriend with him!

I yelled for Mami to come over, and Maria started yelling for her, too. Pedro yipped a few times. She is never happy when we scream for her instead of going to where she is. When she came over, she reminded us again not to do that. Then we asked her what the golf club/hockey stick guys were doing. She knows a lot about art.

Skating on the Frozen Amstel River, 1611 CE · Adam van Breen · National Gallery of Art, Washington, D.C. (The Lee and Juliet Folger Fund, in Honor of Arthur K. Wheelock, Jr.)

"Ah. I'm glad you asked, son," she said. "I was hoping you two would notice that. This first painting, by Hendrick Avercamp, was painted in the around year 1625. You noticed

54

the guy with the colf stick. And in this second painting, which was painted by Adam van Breen in about 1611, there are more people playing colf. These paintings are about 400 years old, and I know you won't touch them."

Maria started laughing and then repeated the name "Hendrick Avercamp" about a million times. I can still hear that in my head. I asked Mami what colf was.

"Well, both of these painters were from Holland, and colf was a popular game back then. That's how the game of golf started. 'Colf' meant 'club' back then, and players would take turns hitting a ball or a rock or something on the ice with a club or stick like you see in the paintings toward some target, and the first player to hit the target would win a point. Why don't the two of you get some clubs from that pile of sticks outside by the storage shed and play some colf in the grass?"

Well, we did that, and it lasted about five seconds—until Maria got mad that I scored the first point and she hit me with her colf in the knee. Mami was too busy to do anything about that, but she shook her finger at Maria. Of course, Maria started to cry, so Mami took us in to look at some other art items. I limped over to where a really fancy cabinet was.

Mami said, "Now let's see if we can find another idea for something you two can do. OK, take a look at this old desk. It's beautiful. It shows two people playing a game called backgammon. It's one of the oldest board games in the world. You see, it's a game of concentration, and the rules are a little difficult to learn..." She stopped talking and looked me, with my bloody knee, and Maria, who was trying to put her elbow in her ear (I dared her to do that earlier). "Never

A Winter Scene with Two Gentlemen Playing Colf (detail), c. 1615 CE · Hendrick Acercamp · The J. Paul Getty Museum, Los Angeles (Digital image courtesy of the Getty's Open Content Program)

mind," she said. "That won't work." She stepped over to another painting, and we stepped with her.

The Backgammon Players, 1861 · Cabinet By Philip Webb, England Painting (in detail) by Edward Burne-Jones · The Metropolitan Museum of Art, New York (Rogers Fund, 1926)

Pedro was outside watching the movers.

"Ah! Here is a good one. It's called *The House of Cards.* This guy is a servant, and he was cleaning up after a party where his boss and other people played cards. The cards are folded in half like that because that would keep people from marking the cards and using them again, which is cheating. And cheating is a very bad thing to do.

He is taking a little break from cleaning to build a house of cards, which takes a very steady hand and lots of concentration..." She stopped talking and looked at Maria, who was twisting her hair around her finger so tight her fingertip was totally white. "Never mind. That won't work either." She stepped over to another painting, and we stepped with her.

"Ok. Here is one by a French painter named Boulogne [Boo-lone- y]. It was owned by Empress Catherine II of Russia!" Maria went "Ooh!" Mami asked, "Can you see anyone cheating in their game?"

She said, "You can see that the guy with the white feather in his hat seems like he doesn't really know how to play the game. The other guys are cheating him. They are all soldiers, and the guy behind the guy with the feather in his hat is probably letting the other soldiers know the numbers on the cards the feather guy is holding. I wonder what game they are playing. You two should go out on the patio and play cards!"

The House of Cards, c. 1737 · Jean Siméon Chardin · National Gallery of Art, Washington, D.C. (Andrew W. Mellon Collection)

Maria and I both groaned. I groaned because, somehow, she always ends up beating me at card games, and she groaned because I groaned.

Soldiers Playing Cards and Dice (and detail), c. 1619 · Valentin de Boulogne · National Gallery of Art, Washington, D.C. (Patrons' Permanent Fund)

"But wait," Mami said. "Look at these other paintings. Here, this one shows fancy people playing cards. They're having a good time..."

Maria asked, "Did an empress or princess own this painting, too?"

"It's so old that we don't really know." "What are they playing?" I asked.

"Art experts think the game they are playing was called Primero," Mami said. "Let's look at these other paintings so I can get some work done." We scooted over a little more.

"This painting is by an American painter, and it shows three men waiting for a stagecoach. This is another scene of people cheating at cards. Can you figure out how we know this? I'll give you a hint. The person standing is not wearing sunglasses. He is wearing the kind of glasses blind people wore back then."

Card Players, c. 1619 · A Student of Lucas van Leyden · National Gallery of Art, Washington, D.C.; (Samuel H. Kress Collection)

Maria and I leaned closer to the painting. One card player looks like a farmer or something, but the other guy in the top hat looks fancy, kinda like the blind man. And...

I shouted, "The blind man is reading a newspaper! He's not really blind! He can see the beard guy's cards, and he's letting the top hat guy know what they are so top hat can win! They're cheats! And look at the name of the newspaper he's reading!"

Mom smiled for a second, but then she frowned when Maria started crying because she was not the one who figured out the painting. Mami tried to calm Maria, but it didn't really work. Then Mami gave us a deck of cards and went back into the kitchen. It was too hot to go out on the patio.

I tried to be nice and deal out cards to Maria to get her

Waiting for the Stage, 1851 · Richard Caron Woodville · National Gallery of Art, Washington, D.C.; (Corcoran Collection)

to stop crying. After a few minutes, we started playing War. Of course, she started winning. Again. I couldn't believe it. I looked around for a way to get out of ending the game with her winning. Two moving workers set a painting nearby. It showed a table that had been knocked over, with cards and gold coins all over the floor. Everyone was helping a lady in a pink dress who fainted. I got an idea.

I started a fake sneezing fit. I sneezed about a hundred times, flapping my arms around and rolling on the floor. Maria looked at the painting, too. I knocked over the deck of cards we were playing with, and I even knocked Maria's cards out of her hands. I made sure to mix up all the cards as I kept on fake sneezing. Maria screamed and started

Waiting for the Stage, (detail) 1851 · Richard Caron Woodville · National Gallery of Art, Washington, D.C.; (Corcoran Collection)

The Faint, c. 1744 · Richard Caron Woodville · National Gallery of Art, Washington, D.C.; (Samuel H. Kress Collection)

crying, but then she suddenly did something that is actually pretty impressive.

We heard mom walking fast in the kitchen toward us. Maria stopped crying, leaned back, and posed just like the lady who fake fainted in the painting. Mom came to us at top speed and then stopped. I started to explain that I just started sneezing and couldn't stop, but Mami put her hand over her mouth and started laughing. She wouldn't stop. Maria opened her eyes to see what was going on.

"I tried to get you two to play a card game nicely together," Mami said. "And then you saw the Longhi [Lon-gee] painting."

The Faint (details), c. 1744 · Richard Caron Woodville · National Gallery of Art, Washington, D.C.; (Samuel H. Kress Collection)

Maria sat up, and I said "What?"

Mami said to me, "Lemme guess. In the painting, it seems like the lady in the pink dress probably knocked over the table on purpose, just like you did, Luis. And then you, María, decided to faint like the pink dress lady to make it look like Luis did something really terrible. Is that right?"

María and I looked at each other. She had us. We were trapped. "Sí," we said at the same time.

"OK," she said to us. "There are two paintings over there side by side by the same artist. Both show people playing cards. Look at them carefully, and, when I come back, tell me what is different about them."

María and I scooted through the jumble of cards to the two paintings.

Three of the card players have really shifty eyes, and the guy on the far right is the only one really looking at his cards.

Right next to the card players painting is another version of it, painted a few years later than the first one. I could tell there are a few differences between the two versions.

Back when these paintings were made, painters would sometimes paint more than one version of a scene so they could sell them and make more money. Also, of course, there were no copy machines or scanners 350 years ago!

Later on, María showed me how she manages to win at cards so much. Essentially, she pays attention to what's going on in the game a lot more than I do. The paintings about games

The Cheat with the Ace of Clubs, c. 1630-1634 · Georges de la Tour · Kimbell Art Museum, Fort Worth, Texas (Alisa Mellon Bruce Fund)

The Cheat with the Ace of Diamonds, c. 1635-1638 · Georges de la Tour · Musée du Louvre, Paris

were all installed, and the exhibition is bringing in visitors from all over South America. Some of my school buddies came and ended up spending the night. We played cards.

Now I wish there was more summer break left because I'm getting really good playing Crazy 8's. I'm learning Spades and Primero, too. It's kinda neat knowing that people have played games all throughout history and all over the world. I guess, in a way, games are important.

Anyway, that's what's been going on at El Museo Cautivador, where I live with my family. I'll write again when the Games art exhibit moves on and we get another exhibit. They're always interesting, as you know.

Your Amigo,

Luis